GW00715879

FROM:

You Rule!

Compiled by Lois L. Kaufman

Illustrated by Donna Ingemanson

PETER PAUPER PRESS, INC.
White Plains, New York

Illustrations copyright © 2004 Donna Ingemanson

Designed by Heather Zschock

Copyright © 2004
Peter Pauper Press, Inc.
202 Mamaroneck Avenue
White Plains, NY 10601
ISBN 0-88088-370-7
Printed in China
7 6 5 4 3 2 1

Visit us at www.peterpauper.com

You Rule!

Take chances,
make mistakes.
**THAT'S HOW
YOU GROW.**

MARY TYLER MOORE

MOMO

It isn't where
you came from; it's
**WHERE YOU'RE
GOING**
that counts.

ELLA FITZGERALD

You **CAN** have it all.
You just can't have
it all at one time.

OPRAH WINFREY

There is a woman at the beginning of all great things.

ALPHONSE DE LAMARTINE

I never said "Well, I don't have this and I don't have that." I said, "I don't have this yet, but I'm going to get it."

TINA TURNER

I've had huge ups and downs
in my life, and I've made some
stupid, stupid mistakes and bad
choices. But no matter what I'm
going through at the moment,
somehow I always think the
future is going to be better,
and somehow it always is.

CHER

There are two or three
performances in your life
that are absolutely on,
where all the planets are lined
up for you and you feel

YOU'RE
INVINCIBLE.

KRISTI YAMAGUCHI

be THE
BEST

All my life I've always had the urge to do things better than anybody else. Even in school . . . I'd want mine to be

THE BEST IN THE CLASS.

BABE DIDRICKSON ZAHARIAS

MOMA

The minute you settle for less than you deserve, you get even less than you settled for.

MAUREEN DOWD

I always wanted
to be **SOMEBODY**,
but I should have
been more specific.

LILY TOMLIN

None of us
suddenly becomes
something overnight.
The preparations
have been in the
making for a lifetime.

GAIL GODWIN

Few things in the world
are more powerful
than a positive push.
A smile. A world of
optimism and hope. A
"YOU CAN DO IT"
when things are tough.

RICHARD M. DEVOS

I want to walk through life
instead of being dragged through it.

ALANIS MORISSETTE

If you obey all the rules,
you miss all the fun.

KATHARINE HEPBURN

I used to feel guilty when I started

becoming successful. I said,

"Why is this happening to me?

I really don't deserve it."

But then I had to say to myself,

"HELL, YES I DO."

I haven't been out there all these

years eating strawberries and cream.

NATALIE COLE

If you have built castles
in the air, your work need
not be lost. That is where
they should be. Now put the
foundation under them.

HENRY DAVID THOREAU

MOMO

I'm **TOUGH, AMBITIOUS,** and I know exactly **WHAT I WANT.**

If that makes me a bitch, okay.

MADONNA

MOMO

You must be able to withstand the
punishment, get up off the ground
after each tackle, and have no fear of
running again at that same defender
who just sent you barreling to the turf.
Eventually you'll wear them down.

MIA HAMM

If you're not looking forward,
you're looking backward or
to the side, and you're going to
smack into something real hard.
ALL LIFE IS CHANGE . . .

UMA THURMAN

Life is **TOO SHORT** to not do whatever you want to do. I've at least made an attempt at investigating everything that's interested me.

LISA LING

I don't deserve
this award, but I
have arthritis and
I don't deserve
that either.

JACK BENNY

We have to do the
best we can. This is our sacred
human responsibility.

ALBERT EINSTEIN

Success didn't spoil me;
I've always been insufferable.

FRAN LEBOWITZ

BE
Brave

You can't be
BRAVE
if you've only
had wonderful
things happen
to you.

MARY TYLER MOORE

Nothing liberates
our greatness like
the desire to help,
the desire to serve.

MARIANNE WILLIAMSON

**Serena and I are BOLD.
We stand out. We have
color. We're STRONG.
We're pretty. We have
personalities. We think
things out. We're SMART.**

VENUS WILLIAMS

Doing the best at
this moment puts you
in the BEST place for
the next moment.

OPRAH WINFREY

I used to want the words,
"she tried" on my tombstone.
Now I want "She did it."

KATHERINE DUNHAM

A hero is a man who
does what he can.

ROMAN ROLLARD

Everyone is a
genius at least
once a year.
The real geniuses
simply have their
bright ideas
closer together.

GEORGE C. LICHTENBERG

It is not enough
to do your best;
you must know
what to do, and then
DO YOUR BEST.

W. EDWARD DEMING

When the time comes [to do something great], just two things matter. How well prepared we are to **SEIZE THE MOMENT.** And having the courage to take our best swing.

HANK AARON

Seize
the
Moment

emanson

MOMO

Young man, the
secret of my success
is that at an early
age I discovered
I WAS NOT GOD.

OLIVER WENDELL HOLMES

Share your fears with yourself
and your courage with others.
You will inspire people to do
things that are incredible.

FRANKLIN D. MILLER,
Green Beret hero in Vietnam war

Nothing in life is to be feared, it is only to be **UNDERSTOOD**.

MARIE CURIE

Obstacles are those things you see when you take your eyes off your goal.

HENRY FORD

There's a part
of me that enjoys
the pressure.
You confront the
pressure, wrestle it,
and then make it
work for you.

ANGIE HARMON

The **SECRET** really seems to be hard work, thorough preparation, detailed knowledge, careful planning, tight organization, strong leadership, dogged persistence, controlled energy, good instincts and the genetic ability to deal.

CHRISTOPHER LEHMANN-HAUPT,
on Donald J. Trump

When someone does something good, APPLAUD! You will make two people happy.

SAMUEL GOLDWYN

I discovered the joy of healthy competition—the kind that makes you strive toward greatness.

CHRISTY TURLINGTON

MOMO

You can become a
WINNER only if you
are willing to walk
over the edge.

DAMON RUNYON

Ideas are like rabbits.
You get a couple,
learn how to handle
them, and pretty soon
you have a dozen.

JOHN STEINBECK

Normal is not something to aspire to, it's something to get away from.

JODIE FOSTER

I have no special
gifts. I am just
PASSIONATELY
CURIOUS.

ALBERT EINSTEIN

I've never had
a humble opinion.
If you've got an
opinion, why be
humble about it?

JOAN BAEZ

Believe in yourself!

HAVE FAITH IN YOUR ABILITIES!

Without a humble but reasonable confidence in your own powers you cannot be successful or happy.

NORMAN VINCENT PEALE

MOMO

The pain we feel when someone
leaves our life is in direct
proportion to the joy they bring
while a part of our life for a few
moments. In my life you made
me feel as if I truly meant
something to someone.

JAVAN

Opportunities multiply as they are seized.

SUN TZU

Some natures are
TOO GOOD to be
spoiled by praise.

RALPH WALDO EMERSON

Every day I get up and look through the Forbes list of the richest people in America. If I'm not there, I go to work.

ROBERT ORBEN

It's always easy to take the route that you know. But it's also boring! You'll never know what you're capable of if you don't try.

SO DON'T BE AFRAID OF FAILURE.

SARAH MICHELLE GELLAR

SHOWING UP
is eighty
percent of life.

WOODY ALLEN

I believe you should never hide your happiness. **IT LIGHTS UP AND CHEERS THE WORLD.** To keep it only for yourself is to lose it.

CELINE DION

MOMO

You may be
disappointed if
you fail, but you
are doomed if
you don't try.

BEVERLY SILLS

I'm extraordinarily
patient provided
I get my own
way in the end.

MARGARET THATCHER

Whatsoever thy hand findeth to do, do it with thy might.

ECCLESIASTES 10:9 KJV

You can never quit.
WINNERS
never quit, and
QUITTERS
never win.

TED TURNER

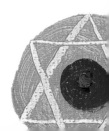

Love me or hate me,
YOU CAN'T
IGNORE ME.

REGGIE JACKSON,
former New York Yankees outfielder

My mother drew a distinction between achievement and success. She said that "achievement is the knowledge that you have studied and worked hard and done the best that is in you. Success is being praised by others, and that's nice, too, but not as important or satisfying. Always aim for achievement and forget about success."

HELEN HAYES

To feel valued, to know, even if only once in a while, that you can do a job well is an absolutely marvelous feeling.

—BARBARA WALTERS

MOMO

[O]nce you've got a certain amount of success, Hollywood goes, "Well, what do you want to do now?" Good question. . . . I guess I gotta grow up and figure out what I want to do.

KEANU REEVES

Nothing can add more power to your life than concentrating all your energies on a limited set of targets.

NIDO QUBEIN

They laughed at Columbus, they laughed at Fulton, they laughed at the Wright brothers. But they also laughed at Bozo the Clown.

CARL SAGAN

The secret of **SUCCESS** is to know something nobody else knows.

ARISTOTLE ONASSIS

I've never sought **SUCCESS** in order to get fame and money; it's the **TALENT** and the **PASSION** that count in success.

INGRID BERGMAN

My formula for success is rise
early, work late, and strike oil.

J. PAUL GETTY

The dictionary is the only
place where **SUCCESS**
comes before work.

AUTHOR UNKNOWN

HAVE fun

It's kind of fun
to do the
IMPOSSIBLE.

WALT DISNEY

MOMO

Perfection is achieved not when
there is nothing more to add,
but when there is **NOTHING
LEFT TO TAKE AWAY.**

ANTOINE DE SAINT EXUPÉRY

MOMO

Things turn out best
for people who make
the best of the way
things turn out.

AUTHOR UNKNOWN

Somewhere out in this audience
may even be someone who will
one day follow my footsteps,
and preside over the White House
as the president's spouse.
I WISH HIM WELL!

BARBARA BUSH